G000168545

Just Where You Left It

Family Rhymes for Modern Times

DAVID ROCHE

With illustrations by Dave Cornmell

Unbound

This edition first published in 2017

Unbound
6th Floor Mutual House, 70 Conduit Street, London W1S 2GF

www.unbound.com

All rights reserved

© David Roche, 2017

The right of David Roche to be identified as the author of this work
has been asserted in accordance with Section 77 of the Copyright,
Designs and Patents Act 1988. No part of this publication may be copied,
reproduced, stored in a retrieval system, or transmitted, in any form or by
any means without the prior permission of the publisher, nor be otherwise
circulated in any form of binding or cover other than that in which it is
published and without a similar condition being imposed on the subsequent
purchaser.

-를 확인, 시내로
주장하였다   -에 따라
절. 조(= chapter)
어떻게 든지. 어떤게 해서라도
유통
부과함   차용의. 자용의

Text Design by PDQ

Art direction by Mecob

Illustrations © Dave Cornmell

A CIP record for this book is available from the British Library

ISBN 978-1-78352-390-0 (trade hbk)
ISBN 978-1-78352-391-7 (ebook)
ISBN 978-1-78352-389-4 (limited edition)

Printed in Great Britain by Clays Ltd, St Ives Plc

1 3 5 7 9 8 6 4 2

To my family, without whom none of this would
be <u>plausible</u>

타당한것같은, 이치에맞는, 그럴듯한
(↔ implausible)
/(특히남을속일때) 그럴듯하게 구는.

(= vraisemblable, admissible)

With special thanks to *chicken!* newspaper, a patron of this book

Contents

Contents

Introduction

As parents, many of us are more than willing to drive our kids around, attend their school events, participate where necessary and generally do our bit. But there is a limit.

For me, the annual school poetry competition was the one. We were all tired of the same old poems being regurgitated, and my eldest son asked me to write one for him to read out. One with a bit more relevance. And more laughs. He didn't win, but "The Poetry Recitation" went down well so I did the same thing the next year for son number two. By the time it was the third son's turn, we won the damn thing.

That winning poem was "Just Where You Left It" and you'll find it here, alongside other poems that reflect on the more amusing aspects of families and modern life. Whether the theme is school rituals or family holidays, breaking the rules, friendship or the many embarrassing faults that parents possess, I have tried to cast a humorist's eye over them all in verse form. And attempted to make them rhyme. Most of the time.

I hope you enjoy them.

David Roche

[Handwritten annotations:]
- attend → —에 참석하다.
- do our bit → 우리의 역할을 다하다.
- being regurgitated → (별내용없이) 반복되는
- with a bit more relevance → 좀더적절하게
- went down well → 망하다, 실패하다.
- By the time → 그때까지, 그때쯤되면, 그시간쯤에는
- alongside → … 옆에, 나란히, … 와함께, … 와동시에.
- verse form → 작성. a composition written in metrical feet forming 률 rhythmical lines. (시의)음보의, 운율의.

1

Just Where You Left It

"Mum, I can't find my shin pads and it's football today.
It's the 3rds v St Wotsits and we're playing away.
They've got that big bruiser who plays at the back.
Where the hell are my shin pads? He is prone to hack."

"They're just where you left them. Why's your memory so poor?
Right under the radiator by the back door."

"Mum, I can't find my door key, I think it's been stolen.
Or maybe it fell from my pocket with the hole in.
So it *is* partly your fault. Can you get me another?
You did it for Daniel, and he's my big brother."

"Conspiracy theory is not a bad call,
But it's right where you left it, on the tray in the hall."

"Mum, I can't find my biro, and it's not '*where I left it*'.
I used it for homework so don't even suggest it.
I left it right here so *you* must have moved it.
It's your fault, it's obvious, and ha!, I've just proved it."

"You've got me. I'm guilty. Arrest me. But wait...
What's that, where you left it, right under your plate?"

So how *do* mums do that? They have a sixth sense
For locating my iPhone or an old fifty pence.
It's the same for our dad too. If he needs the remote,
He just asks our mum and it's *Murder She Wrote*...

"If you got off your backside and looked under the couch,
It's there, where you left it, now mow the lawn." Ouch.

There must be a cheat way that mums win our deference.
They hide stuff, and map it, then learn the grid reference.
They memorise items and their hidden location,
Then have all the answers, like it's their vocation.

"That's right, you believe that while you're all away,
We're just where you left us, doing nothing all day."

cut out for : ~에 적합한. 잘맞는. [a]
ex) After being out of school for so long, I don't think
that I'm cut out for studying anymore.
ex) Maybe I'm just not cut out for this city.

[v] 빠르게 다가가다. :to move quickly toward someone or something

ex) I was so happy to be home that I cut out for
my family the minute I saw them at the airport

Could Do Better

It's the end of term and the school report
Fills me with cynicism. 냉소주의, 비꼬는버릇.

옛날의 In the olden days they'd tell you straight;
Now it's a euphemism.
불쾌한것을 간접적으로 표현하기위한 완곡법.

You've got to learn the secret code
(They don't want to contravene (법·규칙을)위반.위배하다 (= infringe)
The Teachers' Charter), so you must translate
To know what they *really* mean.

For example, they have to describe a child
Even if they don't know them from Adam.
If your child is labelled a "natural leader",
That means they're a right bossy madam.

If they "contribute well to class discussion",
You mustn't get cut up. 소란을 부리다.
If they're "keen to share opinions", ~하기를 간절히 바라다
It just means they won't shut up.   (keen on + N)

If your child is called "creative",
That just means they are a liar.
If they're "dynamic" and "independent",
Their concentration will be dire. 몹시나쁜, 끔찍한. / 대단히심각한, 엄청난.지독

If "active and enthusiastic",
Don't expect a master's degree;
The letters that should go after their name
Are probably ADHD.

· Just anything but that. : 그것만아니면돼. (anything but = never)
· He's used to getting his way. : 그가 원하는 대로 하려고 하세요.
· suppository : 좌약.   6   (= fucked up)
· Your language is seriously effed up : 당신들언어는정말 틀렸네요

"Animated" means disruptive. 지장을 주는, 분열을 일으키는.

A "solitary child" has nits. 멍청이.

"Willing to help" can only describe

A brown-noser, if truth permits.
아첨꾼. (엉덩이에 키스하다보면 불법물이 물어 코가 갈색이 된다고 비유)

"A pleasure to teach" means no trouble.

"Easily upset" means spoilt rotten. → 버릇없는, 제멋대로하는.

If they've "enjoyed the social side of school", → 썩은, 형편없는, 끔찍한
(= terrible)

Class Clown is the name they have gotten.

(= physical education)

If he "enjoys all PE activities", (= definitely)

Then he's deffo a violent thug. 폭력배, 깡패.

If she "expresses herself confidently",

She's cheeky, a smartarse and smug.
건방진, 개구노.   의기양양한, 우쭐해하는 (= complacent)

"Animated" equals disruptive. → (생각·감정을) 분명히표현, 설명하다.

"Articulate" is quite a feat, 솜씨 또렷이말하다 / 발음하다 / 연구하다 /

But it doesn't mean they're good at art.

"Enjoys working in teams" is a cheat.
                    속임수, 사기

If he "knows his own mind", he is stubborn.

"Polite" means his work's not OK.

"Shows interest in her environment"

Means she looks out the window all day.

But remember Winston Churchill,

Whose report said he'd "no ambition";

When he grew up he certainly proved them all wrong...

Do carry on this tradition.

own vs possess

· own → "소유권"이 있는것. 지금당장 나한테 없어도, 나는 그것을
          마땅히 소유하고 있음. 7

· possess → "보유" 한것. 내가지금 가지고 있는것.

My Dad Is Sooo Embarrassing

My dad is sooo embarrassing.
He really is a fool.
He's just bought a Harley
And he thinks that he is cool.

He gets drunk with his sad friends
And then they get all naughty.
What makes me sick and shocked and shamed
Is they're all over forty.

He was God's gift to music,
A rockstar, given the chance.
But it's a total killer
If you ever see him dance.

He also thinks he's sexy
And flirts with the au pair.
I'll never take a girlfriend home
If my dad just might be there.

(서서히) 물러나다. 약해지다. 희미해지다. 빠지다.
His hair's receding rapidly;
It's now just a massive parting.
He combs it over from one side,
A bit like Bobby Charlton.

He also was a sportsman once
And now he's on my side.
The touchline echoes with his yells
And I just want to hide. 메아리치다.

He also thinks he's funny
And tells jokes to all my <u>chums</u>. 친구.
He makes Sid James look classy
With his jests of tits and bums.

But once he was a teenager –
Was a lad, back in his day.
He <u>must have cringed</u> at my grandad
In exactly the same way.
  움츠리다. 움찔하다 (= cower) / 민망하다.

We Have Ways of Making You Eat

School rules are often stupid,
To do with bells and pegs. 못, 핀, 얼룩, 나사.
Shirts must be tucked in trousers
And socks cover half of your legs. → 접어넣은, 단정히끼워넣은

But lunchtime brings The Great Escape.
The Dining Hall is Colditz.
The menu is from World War II
And you cannot eat the old bits.

There's food you won't find anywhere else:
Spam fritters and school liver. 괴기고기야채 튀김
And turkey twizzlers that made their name
Because of Jamie O'liver. 꼬아말아놓은 형태의 것

The dinner ladies patrol the scene
With Gestapo-looking features. 게슈타포. (나치독일의) 비밀국가경찰.
They'll spot any food that's left on your plate
발견하다. And report you to the teachers.

So the people who are legends,
And the ones who set you free,
Are the Food Escape Committee;
"F.E.C." to you and me. 위원회.

We're not talking here about everyday feats
Like faking certain allergies. 솜씨, 위업, 개가.
Or scraping eggs behind radiators
And aversion to the calories.
(무엇을데에내가위해) 아주싫어함, 혐오감.
긁다. 긁어내다.

We're talking total heroes here,
The ones with real worth.

특정부류의)
사람.

The sort who'd dig the tunnels
And then disperse the earth.

흩어버리다, 확산시키다 (= scatter)

Boys like "Goose" McGinty
With a Brussels sprout in his locket. → 싹이나다, 발효하다, 생기다.
Or ones like "Mad Max" Redmond,
Who hid bolognese in his pocket.

Or Josh "White Laces" Russell
With spaghetti in his shoes,
And his pencil case containing
Hidden beetroot for the loos.

→ 밀수하다, 밀반입하다.
But the ultimate name we all revere,
With his smuggling of fish pie,   숭배하다 (= idolize)
Was Ben "The Mole" Carruthers,
Who hid the lot inside his tie.
→ 두더지/스파이/점 (= freckle)

Never was so much smuggled out   밀반출되다. (↔ smuggled in)
By the few who ate so little.
They fought for menus "a la carte"
And for doughnuts with jam in the middle.

푸딩 (= pudding)
"We want puds with custard and cream.
여지 ← We want lychees rather than leeches.   거머리, 거머리같은사람.
(열대성   We know our expedience will improve ingredients
과일의   And we'll fight them on the peaches."
일종)   → 편의, 형편, 방편, 사리.

13

The Poetry <u>Recitation</u>

낭독, 암송, 낭송, 설명, 열거,

My palms are sweaty, my mouth is dry.
There is the stage. I ask myself why
Do I have to do this? It's not fair
To force scared boys to read up there.
Standing alone, when it's your turn.
No text to read, they make you learn.

The first boy up is a nervous <u>wreck,</u> 난파선. 잔해. 엉망진창. 만신창이. 따위
Just stood there on the burning deck.
Parents to right of him. Parents to left of him.
It's all too much and the room starts to spin.
The next boy comes on. Will he be all right?
"Tyger! Tyger! burning bright..."

"That's much more like it," the audience is thinking.
The poor boy spots that his father is <u>winking.</u> (특히 팔꿈치년 살짝) 쿡찌르다.
His mum starts smiling and <u>nudges his</u> brother.
"I did this at school," says the <u>amnesiac</u> mother. 기억상실증. 건망증 환자.
"In fact, I'm sure that I won first prize."
Matilda told such <u>dreadful</u> lies.
　　　　　　　끔찍한. 지독한.
The next one's modern and nobody knows it.
They can't comprehend but nobody shows it.
They prefer verses they learnt as a child:
5박 <u>Iambic pentameters</u>, not text running wild.
　°"*Dulce et Decorum Est...*"
The old ones really are the best.

I'm next.
And I'm scared.

15

There's parents and teachers and sisters and brothers.
The judge seems quite nice but then so did the others.
They're always just so damned <u>condescending</u>; 거들먹거리는, 잘난체하는.
They like your beginning but prefer your ending.
"Kiddies and grown-ups too-oo-oo."
(I'm desperate for the loo-oo-oo.)

I'm up on stage and I know I don't know it.
I can't even remember <u>the poem</u> or <u>poet</u>. 시인
I'm unable to start - my mind is quite <u>hollow</u>. 빈, 움푹꺼진, 쑥 들어간.
If I get the name then the rest just might follow.
Was it Kipling (Rudyard) or Byron (George Gordon)?
Was it T.S. Eliot or W.H. Auden?   (늘게나앉아서) 몸을 웅크리다
                                          → 몹시당황하다. 당황하게 만든다.

"I must go down to the seas again, to the lonely sea and the sky..."
Or anywhere that is not here to just <u>curl up</u> and die. → 호회적벅, 행락지, 호텔
"In Xanadu did Kubla Khan a <u>stately pleasure-dome decree</u>..."   놀이시설
I'd rather be there than standing here or be anyone other than me. (명령판결)
"Jellicle Cats are black and white, Jellicle Cats are rather small..."   등에따라
I'd take being a cat, a <u>spayed</u> one at that, anywhere but in this hall. 명하다
                                                                           결정하
     난소 제거된   → 위풍당당한, 위엄있는 (= majestic)
     불임수술. 중성화수술시킨.   (격식을갖춰느끼고) 우아한, 장중한

Aaaaah.
I remember.
                    (= sound / ring out the knell of)
  통행금지시간.   ↗ ―의 조종을 울리다. ··· 의 소멸 [폐지·몰락]을 알리다.

"The <u>curfew</u> <u>tolls the knell of</u> parting day,
The <u>lowing</u> <u>herd</u> winds slowly <u>o'er</u> the lea, → (= over)
음매하고우는 ←   떼 (= flock)   초원
The dum dum dum de dum de dum de dum."
I can't believe that I don't know line three...

실수하다. 열빠진짓을하다. 실패하다. 망치다.

I struggle on and get through somehow.

I've blown it but feel better now.

My parents grin and stick thumbs in the air.

Do they know nothing or do they not care? 활짝웃다.

The judge will know and will be tougher.

"Nul points" is the right score for a duffer.

멍청이. 뭘 하나도제대로못하는사람.

He's very kind – a small white lie:

He says the standard was quite high.

로마
전설의 ← "Horatius at the Bridge" he rated second. 2위를 차지했다.
영웅

"Beans, Beans" had won (the whole crowd reckoned).

The judge thought not and chose a child

Who delivered, by rote, his Oscar Wilde.

기계적으로. 되풀서.

It's all over. Home seems not far.

The parents chat and won't come to the car.

"I thought you were great," my friend's mum utters.

My dad just says he preferred the stutters. 안절부. 순전부.

He also thinks I deserved a prize,

Proving old age won't make you wise.

So just twelve months 'til we go again.

The stage will be set for mice and men.

I do believe I'll get it right. 올바르게해서 기다. 똑바로하다. 제대로하다.

"I must try harder" is what I'll recite.

I'll work so much – I'll even rehearse

To ensure I change from bad to verse.

Emojis

I guess it started in the Sixties,
Way back with the smiley.
That, and the peace sign,
When they lived the life of Riley.

It's cool, expressive language.
There's one for every mood.
You're got to be a master
If you're going to be a dude.

Your mum won't understand them.
Your dad thinks they are stupid.
They make words <u>redundant</u> 불필요한, 쓸모없는 / 정리해고당한, 실직 당한.
And seem ever so <u>convoluted</u>. 대단히섬세한. 복잡한 / 나선형의, 구불구불하ㄴ

Your parents don't really like them
Cos they are no longer youthful.
They just don't see that if used well,
They are extremely useful.

Emojis help kids make new friends
Through their reading and their writing.
It's so much more productive
Than gossiping or fighting.

They help kids be creative
Like an exclamation mark!
They decorate what you've written
With a dash of panache & a spark.

19

So when you write your stories
Or when you draft your rhymes,
Use these or an emoticon.
They're the signs of the times.

But please don't overuse them
Or lose your vocabulary.
You'll <u>revert to</u> crime, end up <u>doing time</u>,
As a guest of the <u>constabulary</u>.

번역하다. 교도소생활을 하다. 징역을 사다.

(본래상태·습관으로)되돌아가다/ 복귀·귀속 하다.

(영국에서 한 지역의) 경찰대, 경찰지구대.

For Goodness' Sake – Let's Take A Break...

제발, 부디

(= for mercy's sake, for heaven's sake, for Christ's sake, for pity's sake)

When we used to go on holiday
There was a list of *de rigueurs*: (관습·규칙상)꼭 필요한, 어길수없는.
Sunshine, for sure; sand must be gold;
The sea should be azure. azuré 하늘빛의, 푸른.

One hour max from the airport,
All-inclusive (so no tips),
A kids' club for the parents,
Every meal comes with chips.

But these days it all is different.
In Blackpool or in Cannes
The only one essential
Is a high-speed wireless LAN.
근거리통신망. (= local area network)

There has to be a signal,
And by that I mean three bars. 정반에, 영. / 대화를나누다.
There's nothing worse than dull converse
In a family such as ours. 따분한, 재미없는 (= dreary)
→ 조난자. / 버리다, 난파하다.

We need Free Internet Access,
We're not castaways in Wyoming. 와이오밍.
But there's just no way we can afford
The cost of data roaming.

떨어져있는
There's no longer a rule concerning a pool.
The en-suite can be "avocado".
The one thing you just cannot be
Is incommunicado.
(명령령때문에나 자신이원해서) 독인, 공연하는. 의사소통를 단절한

22

And if you think we'll use a cloud,
That makes you such a tosspot. (모욕적인말로) 멍청한, 기분나쁜인간.
And don't think we'll rely on you
For your weak and woeful hotspot.
　　　일,직장,공연시　　　통탄할, 한심한 (= deplorable), 몹시슬픔.
We need 5 gigs, like an Ethernet, 이더넷 (여러대의 컴퓨터를 네트워크를
Can't surf with anything slow-mo.　　　　　행성하는시스템)
We just have to be connected 슬로우모션.
Cos we suffer from the FOMO. 포모증후군. Fear of missing out.
　　　　　　　　　(다른사람은 모두 누리는 좋은기회을 놓칠까봐 걱정되고
　　　　　　　　　　　　　　　　　　불안한 마음)

We're addicted to our smartphones,
Our headphones and computers.
Our line to God is now reliant 의존, 의지 하는.
On 4G wireless routers.
　　　　　　　라우터 (네트워크에서 데이터의 전달을 촉진하는 중계장치)

But our mum is ever so canny 약삭빠른, 영리한.
And she checks it out online.
Before she books the trip, she views
The hotels (and the wine).
　　　　점을찍다 / 여기저기 흩어놓다. 산재하다.
She'll dot the i's and cross the t's,
Her research is abundant. 풍부한 (= plentiful)
Her secret aim is to ensure
Our gadgets are redundant. 불필요한, 쓸모없는 / 해고당한, 실직당한.
(잡고유용한) 도구, 장치.
She knows our dad will never stop
Inspecting work emails.
He'll only glance up from his screen
To gawp at fit females.
··· 을 빤히바라보다. 얼빠진듯이 바라보다. (= gape

23

It's impossible to try and get
The family to <u>desist</u> ··· 를 그만두다 / ex) desist from smoking
And do something nice together   담배를 끊다.
Like a game of contract <u>whist.</u>

카드게임의 하나.

So we're going somewhere new next year.
The idea is to <u>maroon</u> 고동색, 밤색, 적갈색 / 해상에서쓰이는 (조난신호로쓰는) 조명탄.
Us somewhere with no signal at all –
We're taking our break on the moon.

Common Entrance Latin

→ 정신없이, 광적으로, 기를쓰고, 죽어라하고

"You've exactly one hour, you may turn the paper over."
I'm going to need more than my sad four-leaf clover.
My eyes search <u>frantically</u> for anything I've revised.
There's nothing. Not a sausage. Why am I not surprised?

I should have studied harder and learnt my vocab.
I lack motivation unless kicked by <u>a toecap.</u> 구두의앞닫이
I regret all that time spent on my guitar.
It's Latin. I know that. *Res ipsa <u>loquitur.</u>* [연극](…)개막하다.

My mum was so right: "You get out what you put in."
My dad will be mad and will just put the boot in:
"I told you. I told you. But you just didn't <u>listen…</u>" → 작은물방울
Just a <u>*soupçon*</u> of tension and <u>a droplet</u> of *frisson.* → 떨림, 오한, 전율, 몸서리
의심, 의혹, 혐의 / 추측, 예상, 예감. un soupçon de + N : 소량의, 약간의
My dad has a nightmare that is often <u>recurring:</u> 되풀이하여발생하는, 순환하는
He's sitting an exam and his vision <u>is blurring.</u> 흐려진다
He's not studied the subject or taken the course,
But he's now got to sit there and just feel <u>remorse.</u> 후회, 회한.

Thirty years since his school days and he still wakes up
    sweating;
The loss of his youth is not what he's regretting.
He's relieved when remembering his job is <u>a stroll</u> 거닐기, 산책
And <u>relatively</u> relaxing: it's <u>air-traffic control.</u> 항공교통관제소 (작원들)
비교적
Mum's made it quite clear – they don't want any shocks.
"Don't let yourself down like you did in the <u>mocks.</u> (영국에서 공식시 럴전예치는)
If you've learned your lesson, then it's down to revision. 모의고사.
You don't need me to tell you or provide <u>supervision.</u>" 시험공부
감독, 지휘, 지도

26

Dad's motivation was a <u>tad</u> more <u>substantial.</u> (양, 가치, 중요성이) 상당한.

= a little more
조금
크고튼튼한, 단단하지은
(= considerable)

He made a case that was wholly financial:
"Four grand times three terms is twelve grand, oh Max,
Times nine years in all – and that's before tax."

→ work one's ass [butt, arse] off 매우 열심히 일하다.

And just think what we gave up for your education;
Just <u>working my butt off</u> with <u>bugger</u> all vacation.

→ 새끼, 녀석, 놈.

And this is how you thank us, well it was fun while it lasted,
I just can't believe it, you ungrateful bastard!"

He does get excited because it is so expensive,
And to fail big time would be <u>comprehensive.</u> 능력별구분을않는. 한학교에서
But I did pass that test and I am down for Kings 모든수준의학생을지도하는
But I must pass my Latin or the fat lady sings.

Concentrate.

폴리페모스 (외인종 Cyclops의 우두머리), 투옥하다, 감금하다 (= jail)

<u>Polyphemus</u> has imprisoned our hero <u>Odysseus,</u> 오디세우스 (=Ulysses)
A.K.A. Ulysses, whose mate was Dionysius.
Or was it some other? Do they want my opinion?
I know not a <u>jot</u> and can't speak <u>Carthaginian.</u> 카르타고의 (사람)

조금도... 아닌 (부정문을 강조)

And who does need Latin in this day and age?
"It's useful for crosswords," says my <u>pedagogue sage.</u> 교육계의 현자.
But it's a dead language – not useful abroad,
The classes are endless and frankly I'm bored.

So I can't find the answer – I'm lost in translation.
I don't think linguistics will be my <u>vocation.</u> 천직, 소명.
So what *do* I know? Not a lot 'part from these:
Bellumbellumbellumbellibellobellobellabellabella...bellis?

I'm not looking forward to Prize Giving at all;
The only one who failed to make <u>the roll call</u>. 점호, 출석확인.
In front of the Governors, boys, parents and teachers,
I'll <u>be ridiculed</u> as the dumbest of creatures.
비웃음을 살것이다. 조롱당할거다.

Perhaps now's the time to try God and worship?
It's not as if I am requesting a scholarship.
At Latin I'm hopeless. To me it's all Greek.
Time to <u>fall back on</u> my "exam technique".
··· 까지후퇴하다 / ··· 에게대다, 의지하다.

최고의 꿀팁 ←

There are several <u>top tips</u> that we learn in the trade
(Or special insurance as an aid to a grade).
The first and most obvious depends on the seating:
Being next to <u>the boffin</u> is essential for cheating.
(특히연구를 하는) 과학자.

There are other tricks that are far more acceptable
But rely on the marker being very <u>susceptible</u>. 민감한, 예민한 (= impressionable)
At the end of the page where you can't go on far,   / ···들어풍하는, ··· 할수있는
You write: "And in summary, the most important points are…"

(문제나쟁점의) 가장중요한[곤란한] 부분 (=nub)

Then you number each page and end "page 3 of 4",
Then pretend that you lost one: "It was there before…
The whole <u>crux</u> of my answer has now been left out.
A 'B' grade would be fair – benefit of the doubt?"

There's two minutes left and I must finish well,
Just one pearl of wisdom please before the bell.
If only I can pass this I'll never be naughty
But all I recall is Caesar ad sum jam for tea…

That's it. It's all over and now it's the waiting
Until results are published and then it's <u>deflating</u>. (타이어: 풍선등의) 공기를빼다.
I'll not go to Kings now, my chances are slim.   (타이어, 풍선등이) 공기가빠져
I wonder if Dad offered to buy a new gym…?   오므라들다. 기를죽이다.
                                                    (물가를) 끌어내리다. (통화를)
수축시키다.

Two in a Row

Mum and Dad are arguing,
I've heard this one before.
It's just like all the other ones:
An hour (plus encore).

There are several regular categories
For these oral disagreements
And a Richter scale of vigour
From "mild", through "mid" to "vehement".

There's a sort of third dimension
(As well as "decibel")
When it comes the time to measure
Different rates of raising hell.

There's waving of arms, stamping of feet,
One eyebrow raised as quizzical.
There's use of any object to hand
In the dimension that is "physical".

And there's several standard topics
(In addition to who hoovers)
That fall into the category of
Compulsory manoeuvres.

It doesn't matter who works more,
Who contributes higher earning,
When it comes to scrubbing dishes,
Cleaning, washing and the ironing.

And don't start Mum off on cooking,
Dad's "cuisine" just gets her bitching.
We know her views when he chooses to use
Every pan in the damn kitchen.

It's not clever, it's not funny.
It's unnecessary and it's not posh.
My mum does not appreciate
The role of Captain Potwash.

And in line with the ambition,
The reaction gets more hateful.
No Michelin stars in the maison of ours,
Just grumbles from the ungrateful.

So imagine on Mum's birthday
When Dad bought her an appliance.
Mum actually went nuclear –
Q.E.D. Domestic Science.

And when they go out shopping
No earthly force prevents
My dad being tortured by what he describes
As "events, dear boy, events..."

We'll draw a veil across that sharpish,
As a curtain 'cross a rail
In a fashion store changing room
Makes Dad's sense of humour fail.

But it's not just retail therapy
That fails in its description.
Even getting to the shops itself
Is a negative prescription.

Once in the car it's inevitable,
The venue is volcanic.
It summons up the demons from hell
And rituals Satanic.

The road to hell, we're always told,
Is paved with good intention.
But I'm afraid that I'm not paid
For crisis intervention.

It's a guaranteed row, complete dead cert,
Please don't shoot the messenger;
It cannot be stopped even if your name
Is Mr. Henry Kissinger.

Be it reading the map, or refusal
To stop and ask for directions,
Or criticism (however constructive)
And advice with kind corrections.

Who drives is all about fairness,
Dad drives *to* a do, so it's deuce,
Then sinks three drinks in the time an eye winks,
Takes advantage, and gets Mum a juice.

And Mum thinks she drives better,
Dad's so fast she's considered divorce.
But *she* got stopped and has to attend
A Speed Awareness Course.

Let's not get started on DIY
Or other home improvements.
The list goes on a lot longer than
A slow worm's slowest movements.

It's any excuse that sets them off,
They're just like cats and dogs.
I've heard that making up is great
But don't want to imagine the snogs :-(.

So is this a normal relationship
Where "love" sees "all" and conquers?
Or is it really what I suspect?
That both my parents are bonkers.

I'm Not Very Well...

Mum, I think I'm *very* ill,

→ 막대한 (= huge)

I've got a <u>thumping</u> headache.

My <u>glands</u> are all up, I've got a sore throat –

This time it's *not* a fake.

→ 앓은판, 줄, 막. / 버섯의 주름.

→ 영양관 (= lamella, system, nutrient canal, haversian space)

That's so unfair to say that,

How can you be so cruel?

There's things I have to do today.

I *want* to go to school.

But… I think I've got a temperature.

Perhaps we'd better check.

Please go get the thermometer.

Ah! I've <u>cricked</u> my neck…

(목이나 허리에) 근육 경련이 일어나다.

What do you mean impossible?

The reasons could be plenty.

Don't look at me – why could it be

That it now reads 120°?

That's a ridiculous <u>accusation</u>! 혐의, 제기, 비난, 규탄, 고명, 고소, 고발

I'm innocent, can't you see?

You must be mad to think I put

The thermometer in my tea.

It's not as if we've got exams.

I've not "lost another Granny".

I've not "oops, lost my homework, Sir".

Can you please stop saying "<u>uncanny</u>"?

이상한, 묘한 (= weird)

↔ canny : (특히 재계, 정계에서)
약삭빠른, 영리한.

I didn't know that half of my mates
Are sick. Is that what you've found
By ringing all their mothers too?
There must be a bug going round...

What do you mean: "C.O.D. fever"? → The act of staying home
That really is a beauty.   pretending to be sick to
You're taking the mickey, we're not <u>throwing a sicky</u>, avoid school,
That's beyond the *Call of Duty*.   work, social even
                                    거짓병가를 내다   etc. in order to
                                    (pull a sickie)   play Call of Du
                                    (chuck a sickie)

Guidelines for the Sidelines

부업, 사이드라인

When it comes to children's sports
There are rarely purple patches,
And many parents go OTT
Watching their kids' matches.

The same thing happens every week,
It's totally repetitive:
The pitchline parents' masterclass
In how to be competitive.

Four basic types come and watch,
They're totally predictable.
The other factor that they share
Is that they're all despicable.

The first type thinks he knows the rules:
Every tackle deserves a dismissal.
He'd love to be in charge of the game
And so turns on the man with the whistle.

"Oh come on, ref, leave it out!"
His antics get more delirious
Until he becomes the touchline clown.
He just cannot be serious.

Then there's the one who wants to play
And forgets that he's an adult.
He'll trip the other team's flying wing
If it ensures the right result.

38

If "we" score a try in the very last minute
And can win it with a conversion,
He'll try and bribe the touch-judge
Resorting to subversion.

And, of course, there is the worried mum
Whose poor child might get hurt.
You'd think they'd broken their collarbone
When they've peppered their shorts with some dirt.

"Don't touch him, you big bully!"
(She cannot discern fair game.)
She always just assumes the worst:
That it's me they're out to maim.

But the one that's most annoying,
And sadly that's my dad,
Is the one who could do better
And was a *real star* as a lad.

He always brags that in his day
He was the best because... (*zzz zzz*)
Remarkably, the older he gets
The better he once was.

So why don't you all just stay at home
Instead of bringing us shame?
The one thing you can't get in your head
Is that it's only a game!

39

Finding a Mate

How on earth does a Boy meet a Girl
When both want to keep the risk low?
They have to remove all embarrassing moves,
The worst nightmare's their first disco.

It starts long before the occasion (특별한 행사, 의식, 축하 오래 전부터.
When you have to choose how to dress.
Is it white (not a wedding!) or black (no one's dead!)?
It's just like a big game of chess.

기복이심한, 파란만장한 과거, 역사, 이력, / 체크무늬의.
The floor is like a chequered board,
Each side unchartered territory. 특허를받지못한, 면허장이없는 (= unlicensed)
The main objective is to cross the floor 공인되지않은, 불법의.
(And not just to find the lavatory).

The "teams" contain many different types:
There's a Queen – such a precious stone.
The King moves to guard her, one step at a time,
And acts as her chaperone. 한번에
과거 사교행사때 젊은미혼여성을 보살펴주던 나이든여인 / (아역배우처럼 사회
The Queen can do whatever she wants; 활동을하는아동의)
She owns the discotheque. 매니저.
She covers the King, and like a handbrake,
She loves to keep him in check.
그를 억제하다, 억누르다, 감독하다, 방지하다.
주교. There's the Bishop who's ever so confident,
He can move with a pace that is magical.
But he'll usually spoil it because it's the toilet
On the far side that sent him diagonal.

41

(사람이) ‥‥을 다 써버리다. ‥‥이 없어지다. ㄷ물건그을 바닥내다.
/ ‥‥으로부터 도망나오다. 달아나다. / ‥‥ 으로부터 추방하다.

décisif 결정적인
cf. définitif 최종적인, 결정적인.

And the Knight is a curious animal 기사.

Whose first move is always **decisive**. 결정적인 / 결단성있는 ⟷ indecisive.

Then he'll **run out of** bottle, and sidestep (full **throttle**) ➤ 목을조르다. 목줄라죽이다

In case the response is **derisive**. ↳ 회피하다. ⟨몸을옆으로움직여⟩ 피하다. ↓

(dérisoire =) 졍·조소하는 / 극히적은. (cf. à un prix dérisoire (=strang

The Rook is a straightforward person.   헐값으로. Salaire dérisoire 박봉

So it seems, but he's AKA Castle.

He'll be on your wing, then he'll swap with the King.

(He can be a bit of an arsehole.)

(장기의)졸. 느러개 ↰   (=serré)

But the rest of us in the **serried** ranks,

Us **pawns**, we are predictable.

We can start double-time then seem past our prime;

We fear that we're not **delectable**.

아주맛있는. [맛있어보이는. 좋은냄새가나는] / 매력이넘치는.

But if we can keep on going,

Keep a check on our emotion,

If we're confident enough and can just **hang tough**, 완강히버티다. 어려운일을

At the end we can get a promotion.   잘견디다. 잘참고이겨내다.

This allows you to be confident,

You can be whomever you want. 확실하게. 의심할여지없이 (=incontestably

You've got all the moves, which **indubitably** proves

You're a cool cat, and so **nonchalant**. 차분한, 태연한 [무심한](척하는). (= casua
만사태평한.

The reward is you find a partner.

The slow dance is not a disaster. (=rendre) (어떤상태가되게) 만들다. 하다.

The **strains** of *Titanic* need not **render** panic

↙ Because you've become a Grandmaster.

부담. 중압(압박)(감). 압력.

42

Dad Got a C- for My Homework

My dad is so competitive.
He shows it every day.
He has to beat his children
At work, at rest or play.

He tells us it's a "life rule":
The fittest will survive.
He'll never let us win, at all,
As long as he's alive.

And as we kids get older,
And get better in our schools,
I've begun to see Dad struggle,
So he changes all the rules.

But one thing does stay constant
Amongst these legal fads,
And that is my dad is up for it most
Against all the other dads.

And never is that clearer
Than when homework comes around.
Especially if it's a project
And he's on his own home ground.

"Aaah!" he'd say (an ominous start),
"When I was about your size
Mine was fantastic (with sticky-back plastic)
And won a prestigious prize..."

But need some help on the everyday stuff?
It's a different kettle of fish.
His knowledge is partial, a bit out of date,
And his facts are accurate-ish.

"πr^2 is area
and $2\pi r$ circumference."
But joking apart, what he knows by heart,
Has led to misplaced confidence.

When it comes to French it's irregular verbs
That always seem to obsess him.
He'll remember a rhyme, that they did in his time,
And proceed to give me a lesson.

But "La Derniere Vacance" will just leave him askance
If you ask him to help with translation.
He'll revert to type and believe his own hype
With "Monty arrived at the Station..."*

But offer a project with creative design,
Construction or building or such,
And he'll go all manic, and build the *Titanic*,
Taking weeks while saying, "Don't touch!"

Geography is still all Ox Bow Lakes
And glacial U-shaped valleys.
His capital cities are totally wrong.
His dillies are twinned with his dallies.

History is just a handful of dates
That all end with a 66.
The Norman Conquest started it all
When the French came and ruined the mix.

The Great Fire of London was next on his list.
Pudding Lane was aflame at the first. 불타는, 환한, 이글거리는 .
Then he gets all excited: "…that's when West Ham United
Won the World Cup with a hat-trick from Hurst."

With English he's really no help at all
For grammar or for spelling.
It's "i" before "e", except after "c".
"Weird science," I say, and he's yelling.

His Shakespeare is a little sparse;
He only knows *Macbeth*. 여분. → Shakespeare 작의 4대비극중하나. 그주인
"Will these hands ne'er be clean?" (Re-enacting the scene.)
He does make my mum think of death… 연기 . 상연 하여 .

But give him an old shoebox,
And it's *A Night at the Palladium*. 수회선. 보장. 방어울 / 금속원소 Pd .
With yoghurt pots and old loo rolls
He'll build an Olympic stadium.

And you're not allowed to help him
In case you get it wrong.
And maybe – the worst – he may not come first
And some other dad will get the gong.
훈장.

His science is not very good.
His physics not very physical.
Chemistry just leaves him cold
With evidence empirical.
경험에 , 실험에 의거한 , 실증적인 (↔ theoretical)

46

Biology is all very well
With animals, breeding and birth.
He'd much rather see it all on TV,
Watching repeats of *Planet Earth*.

But...

I found one of *his* old school books once
From all those years ago.
His teacher thought he was a dunce!
So much for his ego.   지진아

She'd written in the margin too.   여백에.
She'd marked in big red letters:
"What can I say about your 'work'?
Except you could do better.

"But a curate's egg has some good parts;
At least yours was not long.
Most of the time you don't answer the question,
And when you do, you're wrong."

* *French Irregular verbs:*

Monty Arrived At the station while All the Rest Returned with Tom.
Pa's Moorish Descent gives him a Venturesome *Sort of Nature...*
모험적인, 대담한 (= daring)

Monter, Arriver, Etre, Aller, Rester, Tourner, Tomber,
Partir, Mourir, Descendre, Venir, Sortir, Naître.

The Best Advice

The best advice is simple
And so I'll keep it short.
The only rule you need in school
Is DON'T GET CAUGHT!

The Sports Day

It must be our Sports Day,
It's pouring with rain.
It's got to be cancelled.
They can't do this again.

The car park's quite full
Though it's chucking it down. (침대 아래에) 몸을 내던지다. 내동댕이치다.
People struggling with rugs – 깔개. 양탄자.
If they use them, they'll drown.

The boys milling round, 서성거리다.
Everyone looks dejected, 실의에빠진, 낙담한 (= despondent)
With the obvious exception
If a win is expected.

It's already started.
"Oh no, are we late?
I did say to you, darling,
We must leave by eight."

"But no, you knew best,
Just one more minute in bed.
Half an hour with the paper
And look where it led." 연결되다. 이끌고가다. 안내하다.

We start with the sprints: 전력질주.
"On your marks, get set, go…"
We wait for the gun –
Does it work? Of course, no.

This causes a problem
for the formidable females,
Reading their stopwatches
As if they were emails.

It looks expertly done
With them all on their ladder,
But the order's all wrong
And the timekeeping badder.
                    worse

"Just watch out for smoke
From the gun," say the leaders
As the boys run right past them
At one hundred metres.

They invent the times
And are all sworn to silence.
   ─에   맹세하
It's not a school record,
If it was there'd be violence.

The funny thing is
That it just doesn't matter
Because all of the parents
Are having a natter.
              수다 (= chat)

They're not paying attention
To the field or the track.
They're stuffed in the grandstand
   너무 배부른   야외경기장 관람석
Right up at the back.

Then the sun deigns to visit.
Let battle commence!
It's a sprint with the rugs 전력질주
To the hill by the fence.

Who's got the best *milieu?* 사회적환경 (= background)
Have we got the best scene?
We can't see the races
But can see and be seen.

The main event is now on.
Start the parade.
It's time for the picnic.
Is it bought or home-made?

It's a delightful paté.
"Says canard on the lid."
Or, imagine a pork pie
Or Spam (God forbid).

Sympathy here is the
Worst of the goads. 자극. 막대기 / 들들볶다.
"No, do help yourself.
We've absloootly loads." 짐. 화물. (=cargo). 싣다.

가차없는
She's ruthless, a sadist
Who kills with a crumb. 부스러기. 작은것. 소량.
Who is this assassin? 암살범.
Competitive Mum.
경쟁하는. 경쟁심강한. 뒤지지않는. 경쟁력있는.

"Going on <u>hols</u>?" holidays.

"Yes, we're off to Mauritius."

경주 <u>The stakes are up high</u> : 내기판돈이 크다. 위험성이 크다. 리스크가 크다.

And it's now getting <u>vicious</u>.
　　　　　　　잔인한. 사악한. 공격적인.

All through this time,

Way back on the track,

They've been running the races

And not looking back.

"Is it nearly all over?"

All parents are hoping.

Then they bring out the hurdles

And we all end up moping.

Because they all need arranging,

Each one in its place,

Just so some short kid

Can fall flat on his face.

　　　　　　짜증나는　　(작은것들을 다루거나　소소한 일들을 해야해서)

And they're so <u>bloomin' fiddly</u> 성가신.

With extendable legs

And those horrible, stubborn,

<u>Retractable</u> pegs. 말뚝. 밧줄. 못. 꽂이.

(몸통속으로) 집어넣을 (오므릴)수있는.

Hang on! It's the relays.

We know they're on last.

And then it's the presents

And it'll be in the past.

But then there's the waiting.
"Mum, can't we just go?
I didn't win anything."
"Well... you just never know."

There's speeches and prizes,
A Victor Ludorem
For some smart-arse kid
Whose parents adore him.

But not only that,
He got another four prizes
And three silver cups
The size of Devizes.

The family stagger 비틀, 휘청거리다. (= totter)
Under the weight of their booty. 전리품, 노획물(= loot) / 엉덩이 (= buttocks)
We wave with fixed grins
(And don't think they're snooty).
　　　　　　　　오만한 (= snobbish)

It's a nice happy ending
To a very long day though.
As they get to their Jaguar,
We get to our Polo.

We've endured four whole hours
But it had to be worth it
Just to see that their car
Had a puncture. How perfect.
　　　　펑크, 구멍 생겨 (= flat)

No Room for Us on the Bus

A full day at school is quite long enough,
But it's often the journey that makes it so tough.
It takes me an hour to go door to door.
OK, I exaggerate, but it often feels more.

→ (특히 짧은 시간 동안 무엇을) 제자리에 두지 않다. (그래서 찾지 못하다)

The commuting *to* school is not very funny:
You <u>mislay</u> your pass and you've forgotten your money.
You beg and you borrow from a mate for the fare,
And he wants it with interest – any kindness is rare.

The bus is all full when it comes to your stop.
You decide to walk up the hill to the top.
And <u>smack</u> in between the two stops is the bit
Where you are when the stupid bus passes you. Shit!

└ (손바닥으로, 특히 벌로) 때리다 (= spank)

So you start to run but the driver ignores you.
The schoolkids on board make faces that bore you.
The grannies, in *your* seat, peer through their glasses,
Taking rides, just for fun, on their pensioners' passes.

But on the way home…

폭력배, 깡패.   줄을 서다. 이루다.

Our uniform's worse than a team's tribal dress.
It invites <u>thugs</u> to <u>line up</u> and make it a mess.
Just whose idea was it to make us a target?
To be victims for every bully and large <u>git.</u> 재수없는 멍청한 놈.

(특히 많은 사람들 사이를 지나가면서) 집중 공격 [비판]을 받다.

We're <u>running the gauntlet</u> right from the school gates.
                          지점
To get to the bus stop, you must go with your mates.
                                                수적으로
As outsiders we have to <u>outnumber</u> the locals; … 보다 수가 더 많다. 우세하다.
There's safety in numbers when you're <u>up against</u> <u>yokels.</u>

── 을 맞닥뜨리다.   촌놈. 시골뜨기. 무지렁이.

(= be faced with. be confronted with [by].
                                        come upon [across],)

throw down the gauntlet 도전을 하다.

take up the gauntlet 도전에 응하다.

They're after your Oyster, they're after your mobile.
You must have them hidden and keep a low profile.
Just wear your school shoes, and bury your trainers.
Keep anything valuable in <u>padlocked</u> containers.
땡뽕이자물쇠로잠긴

When you do get home safely, without the <u>collision,</u> 충돌사고.
Your reward is an hour of Geogers <u>revision.</u> 복습/시험공부
You forget to get back the <u>quid</u> you did borrow, 파운드.
And, joy of joy, it's the same thing tomorrow.

Social Not-Working

My mum's signed up to Facebook.
She wants to be a spy.
There's only one reason, and it's total high treason:
She can only have signed up to pry.

My mum's always trying to poke me.
She wants to be my "friend".
My privacy setting is clearly not letting
Her see what I do at my end.

I'm currently "in a relationship" –
My kindred soul's a sweet talker.
My mum has not met them (to personally vet them),
That's why she's a wannabe stalker.

The photos are the worst thing;
She could see just what I am doing.
It's my personal dominion (InMyHumbleOpinion),
Would she mind if she saw the tattooing?

She's only trying to protect me (she says)
From dirty old perverts and freaks.
But that's just too cosy, she's just being nosy,
And Facebook is not for antiques.

It started when I was texting;
She'd find my inbox and peruse it.
So I'd smartphone an upgrade and confuse the old maid:
With no scoobie on just how to use it.

Mum's ancient, from the Stone Age,
Has no idea what I <u>meme</u>.
She'll never receive a TBH
Cos she's from the Age of Steam.

Mum should never go on Snapchat.
She never will succeed
To understand the habitat
Of Pinterest or BuzzFeed.

She then downloaded WhatsApp
And signed up to Instagram.
There was too much of an age gap;
She tried to send a telegram...

YouTube, Netflix and Spotify
Are OK – I gave her that <u>titbit</u> –
But she's never, ever sharing with me if
I'm showing a pulse on Fitbit.

So stay on your LinkedIn and Saga Zone
And don't even think about Twitter.
Your excuses are waffle (you should see me just ROFL).
You look old and twisted and bitter.

So don't wonder what I do at bedtime
Or try watching what I do upstairs.
It's *my* room and *my* mates – you'll *never* meet my dates –
Just trust me. Or I'll check *your* affairs...

Prize Giving

I wish my parents wouldn't come.
I wish they'd stay away.
It's just no fun, when you've won none,
To attend a No Prize Day.

But they do insist on being there;
It's one they wouldn't miss.
Mum's all dolled up, Dad's just got up
After a Friday on the piss.

The Governors' procession is a miserable line;
Grim-faced they walk up the aisle
Like some death march, all stiffness and starch;
The setting is getting hostile.

Then just when you thought that it couldn't get worse,
The orchestra comes in crashing.
With scraping and bowing, the music is going,
To get a damn good, metaphorical thrashing.

The Headmaster's up next, in predictable form.
It's all "journeys" and "launch pads" and "goals".
We "must act our age" as we've "reached the next stage".
And "...in the next act we play adult roles".

The fathers of kids make a penitent show;
Heads bowed indicate they're respecting...
But they're bluffing – moreover, they're completely hungover.
It's their emails, in fact, they're inspecting.

It's time for the ranking; who's better than whom?
Did you get to your preferred school?
Or were you just beaten to Westminster and Eton?
Is there foolproof proof you're a fool?

The Head Boy is given The Headmaster's Prize.
The wimp wins The Chivalry Cup.
The thug (no decorum) wins the Victor Ludorem.
Is this all not predictable? Yup.

It's endless as queues parade to the stage.
Their parents all strain for a look
As Tarquin or Sophie pick up the maths trophy
And collect the inevitable book.

It's time for the speech from the celeb who's come,
She's one of the kids' auntie's friends.
We'd been looking forward, but now aspire doorward,
As the bore has the floor with no end...

Then it's finished, it's tea and cucumber sarnies.
I'm an "old boy" at 13 already.
The mums can just prattle on, tittle and tattle,
While the dads (*sotto voce*) ask, "Ready?"

When I look back I'll think what was that all about?
Was it character-forming or scam?
But all that does matter is my old Alma Mater
Taught me how to pass an exam.

Frankly, Mrs Butler...

"If I can have a quiet word…"
Is generally how it's started.
The expression on Headmaster's face
Is the same as if I'd farted.

Then comes the opening gambit
When you've missed your third appointment:
"Well, frankly, Mrs Butler… "
With that look of disappointment.

"The staff attend in their own time;
It's outside of normal hours.
Most parents want to get feedback
On their loved one's learning powers.

"And your son has shown *real* talent
With his progress on the triangle,
But you missed the concert once again.
What excuse, this time, can you fangle?

"His rhythm is better and his phrasing is fine.
He has worked very hard on his phonics.
If you showed the same commitment as him,
Then you'd not reek of three gin and tonics.

"Your son at recent exhibitions,
Showed proficiency in Art Deco,
But you missed the talks while unpopping corks
Of some delightfully chilled, dry Prosecco.

"So we seem to have a big problem.
This evening is just a sample.
Your son has no chance," (he looked quite askance),
"When you set such a rotten example.

"The school has a reputation
That it's important we protect.
Our children are ambassadors
And they treat us with respect.

"And most of the parents are a delight.
They're active and do get involved.
But there are one or two, and I'm looking at you,
Who are problems that remain unresolved.

"You're with us or you're against us,
And on trust this relationship's built.
And what part of the fun is, the fact that your son is
Related, just makes you feel guilt.

"I want you to go home and have a good think;
The Lord does work mysteriously.
And when you get there do not have a drink.
Be responsible and please take this seriously."

So I return home all shameful and downcast
And wait for my husband to come.
There's no dinner awaits him; I'm a terrible wife
As well as a terrible mum.

But at last he gets back from his long day at work.
Takes his tie off before it can throttle.
"What a day," he utters, and then to me mutters:
"I'd better go get us a bottle…"

Bully for You

Have you ever been to the tuck shop,
Bought your sweets, then been confronted?
The biggest thug stands in your way
And makes you feel quite stunted.

He wants you to give him your Mars bar,
He'll batter you – or worse, maybe.
For him it's no problem, it's as easy as
Taking candy from a baby.

But you must learn to defend yourself –
Stand up and face the music.
Even if you've a tear and you have a fear
That threatens to make you feel sick.

You cannot be a pushover,
You have to be more furtive.
Tread the fine line, stiffen your spine,
And learn to be assertive.

"Sticks and stones may break my bones.
Names can never hurt me."
But bullying can be emotional
And do more than disconcert me.

Bullying can take many different kinds:
There's physical, verbal and cyber,
Psychological too, and unless you
Stop it early you'll become a subscriber.

The bully must have a target,
And they prey on anyone different.
But don't rise to the bait; just learn to wait
And try to be indifferent.

So imagine that you are ticklish
And they're asking – and testing – but when
It's your turn just get through the first time
And you'll find it won't happen again.

And a bully doesn't like it
If you push back and try to stand tall.
You've heard the expression that sums them all up:
If they're bigger, the harder they fall.

A bully is someone who is suffering themselves;
They may well have been maltreated.
They are often victims and then take it out
On others, and so it's repeated.

So next time a bully tries picking on you
Don't let them become <u>abusive.</u>
They thrive when damning diversity.
Be their Kryptonite – and be inclusive.

Thank You, Baby Boomers

There's a group that suffers from rumours
And deserve our condemnation:
They're called the Baby Boomers –
The Most Selfish Generation.

So just who are this greedy lot?
They're your grandpa, they're your nan,
And, if a late starter, it's your dad,
Because he's an older man.

They were born after World War II
(After nineteen forty-five),
From then up to the Sixties
To round about '65.

They lived in what's called a "golden age",
They'd never had it so good.
They never fought in a Great War;
Had the ideal childhood.

Their teens were the '60s and '70s
It was all a haze of smoke.
Their cigarettes were Lebanese,
They taught the world to sing with a Coke.

Then they went to university.
Paid for on a full grant.
They knew nothing of adversity.
They were left a few grand by some aunt.

Their first job was in advertising
(At uni they'd done journalism).
The interview was a rubber stamp.
Their dad knew the boss. Nepotism.

Then they got on the property ladder:
A first flat with a generous mortgage.
No snakes in this game, no poisonous adder,
Always gains and never a shortage.

Then maybe got married, and then had a kid.
The nice flat would no longer suffice.
"We'll sell it and move to a much bigger place –
Oh look, it's doubled in price!"

So what did they have, these "wunderkinds"?
NHS and North Sea Oil;
They were sent all sorts of favourable winds,
Any poo just enriched the soil.

They lived in consumer wonderland
Had long holidays, wider travel.
The Continent replaced Sunderland.
Their driveways were covered in gravel.

This was the era of invention,
They put a man upon the moon.
At home they bought a dishwasher
To wash three sizes of spoon.

Well, lucky old you...

You look back and become sentimental.
The truth is inconvenient:
Your damage went environmental.
Don't expect us to be lenient.

So you lived a life of plenty
In relative ecstasy.
The luxury Cognoscenti.
So what now is your legacy?

Unlike you we pay for our unis,
U turned on us – tuition fees!
We now take out a mortgage
Just to get our measly degrees.

Then we look for gainful employment,
Find the market is like the slave trade.
And, much to our enjoyment,
Become interns even though it's unpaid.

And, you stopped building houses.
The votes from the NIMBYs were carried.
So we live in a bedsit with spouses,
Though we can't afford to get married.

And Lord help us if we are sick,
Get a tumour so big our pants split.
As the greedy and needy who got rich quick
Had the NHS finance it.

You bought property from your vast probate.
Bought to let and ripped off your lodgers.
Then diddled the tax due from your estate;
You don't need a yacht to be dodgers.

And you lot will live forever,
No stress or hypertension.
The ultimate "whatever"
With your gold-plated, inflated pension.

You're off on your cruises, in your upgraded classes.
Inheritance spending's not hard.
We're thankful our taxes pay your bus passes;
The world is your Oyster Card.

Then, as if that wasn't enough,
From the era that has all and wrecks it,
You decide that it's really too good for us
And vote in favour of Brexit.

So what becomes of Generation Z,
Or, as we're sometimes called, iGen?
You lived in clover, we've got your hangover,
We're poorer than you were at 10.

But you've set us an example,
You had it all and blew it.
We agree that we've learned, if my friends are a sample,
Just exactly how NOT to do it.

So now we'll work to clean up your mess.
There's a truth that we've learned to believe.
The *Me, Me, Me* ethos will be buried with you.
It's better to give than receive.

And one specifically for the parents, no matter how old your kids are...

If You Bill It, They Will Come

Let's face it:
When your kids
Are in their teens
They prefer their machines
To any of their genes.

Their parents
Are, at best,
A punishment.
Handbrake, impediment,
Extreme embarrassment.

Too "grown up",
No time for
Your holiday:
A fun-packed getaway,
A week in Colwyn Bay?

After school, a gap year?
They want somewhere tip top.
Backpack, hiking, flip flops, party island
Hostels, beer, hip-hop, Ibiza, Thailand...

No postcards, no text news,
No info, just a blur.
A call: dosh scant, transfer, I'll pay you back.
Are you OK? Banter. A heart attack?

Then just about the time
They can't afford full board
Or a smorgasbord at home or abroad,
It's all about what parents can afford.

Throw money at the problem if you can.
They'll make time if there's beaches and suntan.
In order to book a three-line whip vacation,
Just focus on location, location, location.

Skegness, Southend-on-Sea and Bognor Regis
Just do not cut the mustard as prestigious.
But offer skiing in Whistler, Zermatt or Gstaadt,
And I think you'll find you're holding the trump card.

Try Copacabana, Seychelles or Aruba;
Galapagos Islands, Maldives – for some scuba.
A city break might make the grade, if you pitch it right:
New York, Shanghai, Cape Town or Laos (and not an economy flight).

So they really will come if you cough up enough.
If you do not dig deep, then expect a rebuff.
The time-honoured words of the Beatles were really just hype:
That "money can't buy you love" is clearly just tripe!

Bless their little cotton socks...

About the Author

David Roche was born in London, got a <u>faintly grubby</u> degree in psychology at Durham University, and then got married far too young. Thirty years later, he and his Finnish wife have three sons in their twenties. David has worked, for what seems to him an inordinately long time, as a director of HMV, Waterstones, Borders and Books etc., and also in publishing at HarperCollins. He now lives in Kingston upon Thames and has several roles related to books and writing. This is his first book.

@davidlrroche

Acknowledgements

I'd like to thank Scott Pack for putting up working with me in many of the same companies for the best part of twenty-five years and still agreeing to edit this book; to Dave Cornmell for his fantastic illustrations that bring the poems to life and for putting up with my endless, pedantic requests; to everyone at Unbound for making the book happen and for it looking so lovely; to Rokeby School for inspiring me to write the first poem in order to ameliorate the boredom of attending repetitive Poetry Recitation evenings as a parent; to Mr Philips, the English teacher there at the time, who was both understanding and appreciative of my anonymous efforts; to my sons who performed a few of these poems with great gusto and even prize-winning form; to my wife for kicking my arse when needed; but most of all to everyone who supported my book by pledging and making it happen, and particularly to the book's patron, *chicken!* newspaper and Ken Wilson-Max – I do hope that you enjoy it.

Supporters

Unbound is a new kind of publishing house. Our books are funded directly by readers. This was a very popular idea during the late eighteenth and early nineteenth centuries. Now we have revived it for the internet age. It allows authors to write the books they really want to write and readers to support the books they would most like to see published.

The names listed below are of readers who have pledged their support and made this book happen. If you'd like to join them, visit www.unbound.com.

Andrew Anderson
Andy Arundell
Paddy Atkinson
John Auckland
Richard Barham
Emma Beaumont
John Beavan-Vaughan
Meera Bedi
Clarey Bee
John Bond
Doug Bone
Emma Bourne
Tim Brownlow
Duncan Bruce-Lockhart
Eugene Buckley
Cortina Butler
Joanna Carpenter
Calum Chace
Ed Christie
Nicholas Clee
Richard Colyer

Stephen Conway
Lucy Cooper
Simon Coughlin
Peter Cullinan
Joseph Cunningham
Beverley Davies
Eliza and Martha Davies
Tim Davies
Paivi Dubois
Plum Duff
Tanya Dunbar
Pat Edney
Lisa Elder
Geoff Ellis
Joanna Ellis
Paul English
Tracey Flashman
Josette Fontaina
Charlie Foreman
Susanna Frayn
Minna Fry

Marzia Ghiselli
Martyn Gibbs
Mary Gibson
Alan Giles
Rina Gill
Corinne Gotch
Jonathan Gould
Eric Green
Gordon Gregory
Stephane Groud
Lucy Hale
Alex Hardy
Giles Harris
Henrietta Heald
Fran Hellawell
Jo Henry
David Hicks
Alex Hippisley-Cox
Jamie Hodder-Williams
Marc Hull
Michael Humphries
Hermione Ireland
Carmen Jansz
Annie Jenkins
Jane Johnson
Paul Johnson
Trevor Johnson
Simon Juden
Aisha Kalkisheva
Heikki Kari
Ilkka Kari
Suzanne Kavanagh
Annette Kelly

Fiona Kennedy
Dan Kieran
Jasmin Kirkbride
David Kohn
James Kyle
Raili Lampola
Maxine Lister
Karen Little
Jonathan Lloyd
Helen Loeb
Melanie Loeb
My Ly
Stuart Macdonald
Seonaid Mackenzie
Koukla MacLehose
Kerr MacRae
Steve Mahoney
Riku Makinen
Riikka Mäkinen
John Makinson
Claire Malcolm
Gautam Malkani
Sarah Massey
Roger Mavity
Carolyn Mays
Helen McAleer
Neil McEwan
Pat McGroin & Mike Hunt
Philomena McManus
Lucy Metcalfe
Lesley Miles
Lisa Milton
John Mitchinson

Deena Mobbs
Alyson Montgomery
Luke Morley
Toby Mundy
Hamzah Munif
Caroline Murphy
Heidi Murphy
Tuija Murray
Carlo Navato
Michael Neil
Beverley Newman
Kes Nielsen
Meredith Niles
Federica Nistri
Beryl O'Brien
Natalie O'Neill
Tom Owens
Scott Pack
Bryan Park
Tim Parrack
Jane Partridge
James Paul
Alexandra Pett
Justin Pollard
Miles Poynton
Ross Prideaux
Caroline Proud
Jake Pugh
Aapo Rekiaro
Alice Rendle
Claire Reynolds
Anthea Robertson
Ben Redmond Roche

Chris Roche
Daniel Redmond Roche
Max Roche
Onna Roche
Patrick Roche
Stuart Rowe
Barbara Rozycki
Anita Russell
Trudi Ryan
Mark Samuelson
Ruth Savill
Katriina Serenius
Justin Serrano, Jr.
Hugh Shanks
Justine Solomons
Tom Stevenson
Peter Straus
Roger Tagholm
Jane Tappuni
Jacks Thomas
Stephanie Thwaites
Nick Turnbull
Anni Vartola
Malcolm Wall
Glen Ward
Fiona Wheeler
James Wood
Alex Woodhouse
Hamish Woodhouse
Linda Wootton
Andrew Wynd
Alan Young